A DEMOGRAPHIC LOOK AT TOMORROW

Harold L. Hodgkinson
Center for Demographic Policy
Institute for Educational Leadership

June 1992

ACKNOWLEDGMENTS

Special thanks must go to the Carnegie Corporation of New York and most especially Ms. Vivian Stewart for their support of the Institute for Educational Leadership's Center for Demographic Policy. Their continued interest in changing demographics and education is greatly appreciated.

Janice Hamilton Outtz, Associate Director of the Center for Demographic Policy, was responsible for research, editing and production of the report. I am also grateful to Anita M. Obarakpor, Program and Research Associate in the Center, for her research assistance; Louise Clarke, Chief Administrative Officer, for administrative support; and, of course, Michael Usdan, President of the Institute for Educational Leadership, for his continued support of the Center.

Errors of fact or interpretation, however, remain the responsibility of the author. This publication was prepared with funding from the Carnegie Corporation of New York. The opinions expressed in this report do not necessarily reflect the views or the positions of the Carnegie Corporation of New York.

Harold L. Hodgkinson

Copies are available by writing to:

Publications Department
Institute for Educational Leadership
1001 Connecticut Avenue, N.W. Suite 310
Washington, D.C. 20036
(202) 822-8405
(202) 872-4050 (FAX)

Prices are: 1-9 copies $12.00 each
              10-24 copies $10.50 each
              25+ copies $9.00 each

Cover Design: Cultural Projections Unlimited

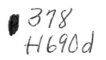
TABLE OF CONTENTS

A DEMOGRAPHIC LOOK AT TOMORROW

Tomorrow is in part an extension of today's trends. We can be very confident in predicting changes from 1990 to 2000, and a trifle less confident in predicting changes from 2000 to 2010. A first year graduate student in demographics can project the population of the United States for the year 2000 with less than a one percent error rate. A Nobel laureate in economics, on the other hand, would be in great trouble forecasting the Gross National Product for the year 2000 with a 10 percent error rate. The point of this brief paper is to use the 1990 census data as a jumping-off point to investigate changes that are very likely to occur during the 1990 to 2010 period. Our first task for this demographic look is to examine the 1980 to 1990 trend lines from census data.

THE UNITED STATES IN 1990

Let's look first at some overall growth rates for various racial and ethnic groups in the United States. The nation increased by 22.1 million persons, reaching a total of 248.7 million in 1990. Different racial and ethnic groups increased at vastly different rates, as can be seen in Table 1. How the United States population in 1990 was made up by race and ethnicity can be seen in Table 2.

States and Regions

Just as the different racial and ethnic groups grew at different rates, so did the different regions throughout the U.S. Ninety percent of the growth in the U.S. happened in the south and west, while only three states got half of the nation's growth: California, Texas and Florida. Never in the 200-year history of census-taking have only three states had half the *nation's* growth. As a result, California, Texas and Florida picked up 14 seats in the U.S. House of Representatives; seats that were given up by Pennsylvania, Michigan, Ohio, Illinois (two seats each) and New York (which lost three seats) and several other states which gave up one seat each.

Table 1	
Percent Change in U.S. Population by Race and Ethnicity, 1980-1990	
	1980-1990 Increase
Total, U.S.	9.8%
White, non-Hispanic	6.0%
Black	13.2%
Native American, Eskimo or Aleut	37.9%
Asian or Pacific Islander	107.8%
Hispanic (of any race)	53.0%
Source: U.S. Bureau of the Census.	

Table 2		
U.S. Population by Race and Ethnicity 1990		
	(000) Number	% of Total Population
U.S. Total	248,710	100.0
White, non Hispanic	187,137	75.2
Black*	29,986	12.1
Native American, Eskimo, Aleut*	1,959	0.8
Asian or Pacific Islander	7,274	2.9
Hispanic (of any race)	22,354	9.0
*Includes a small number of Hispanics. Source: U.S. Bureau of the Census.		

Growth in the U.S. was bi-coastal as well, with Georgia, the Carolinas and Virginia also making large gains in population. The heartland and mid-

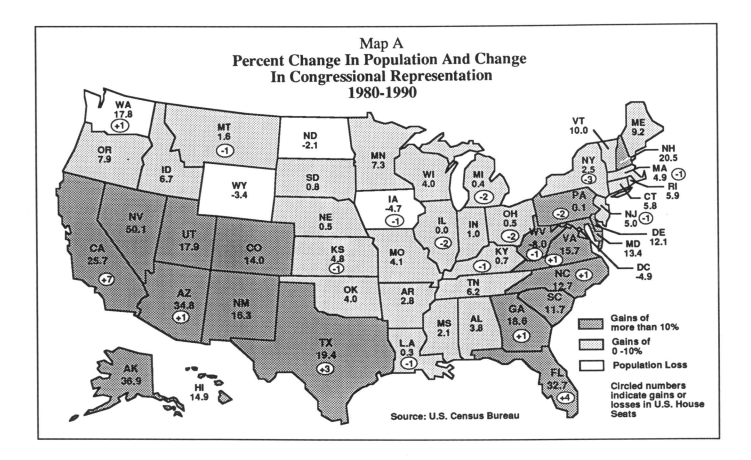

Map A
**Percent Change In Population And Change
In Congressional Representation
1980-1990**

Source: U.S. Census Bureau

Gains of more than 10%
Gains of 0 -10%
Population Loss
Circled numbers indicate gains or losses in U.S. House Seats

Atlantic states were the overall losers. By the next census, Texas will move into the second largest spot, and the Empire State of New York will drop to third. This decline will cost New York over one billion dollars in federal funds which are distributed to states based on their population. Map A (above) shows the gainers and losers by state as a result of the change in population between 1980 and 1990.

It is anticipated that the population growth rates will continue at their uneven pace through the next decade with concentrations in the southeast and west regions (see Map B on next page -- Projections of the U.S. Population, 1988-2000).

Politics

By the year 2000, the Congressional Research Service has stated that California will have 50 seats in the House of Representatives, Texas will have 34 and Florida will have 28, for a total of 112 seats in the

three states. That could be enough votes to defeat legislation introduced by any of the other states, regardless of party. (The U.S. Constitution requires us to hold a census every decade in order to revise the House of Representatives to accurately reflect the population.)

Concentration

In 1990, nine states made up half of the U.S. population: California, New York, Texas, Florida, Pennsylvania, Illinois, Ohio, Michigan and New Jersey. But as we can see from Map A, six of the nine states are not increasing much at all. The "new South" of Georgia, Virginia and North Carolina may move into the top nine states by the next census. State rankings by population are crucial to the amount of federal block grant funding they will receive. The larger a state's population, the more dollars it receives.

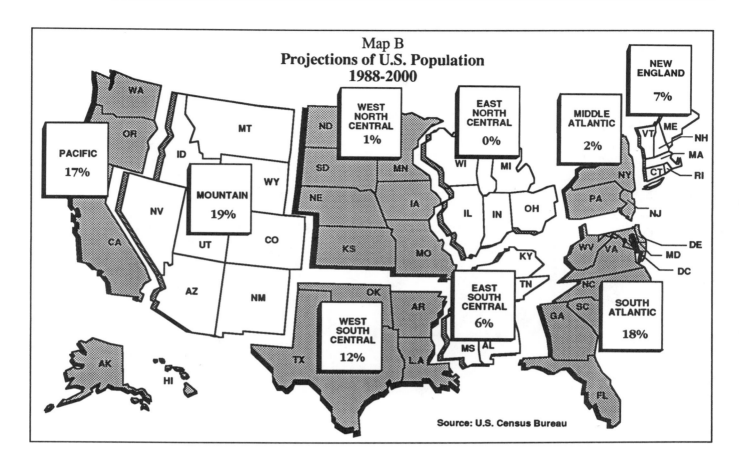

Map B
**Projections of U.S. Population
1988-2000**

Source: U.S. Census Bureau

The states that are growing most rapidly tend to be states with a high percentage of minorities, especially minority youth. By 1995, the trend will be quite clear (see Map C on page 4 -- Minority Public High School Graduates).

Prisoners and Dropouts

Some other key developments happened during the 1980 to 1990 period. The fastest growing group in the U.S. was prisoners, up 139 percent, from 466,371 in 1980 to 1,115,111 in 1990. We now have a higher percentage of our population behind bars than any other nation. A black male in the U.S. is seven times more likely to be in jail than a black male in South Africa. Black men, who make up just six percent of the U.S. population, are now three percent of college student enrollment and 47 percent of America's prison population. Prisoners cost the taxpayer an average of $22,500 a year (as of fiscal year 1991), a very poor investment, as 73 percent of all prisoners released are back in jail within three years. Eighty-two percent of America's prisoners are high school dropouts. The best way to reduce crime rates is not to build more jails but to reduce the high school dropout rate, giving youth a "straight" alternative.

Family Shifts

The American family made some striking changes during the last decade. The "Norman Rockwell" family - a working father, housewife mother and two children of public school age - was SIX percent of all households for most of the decade. Data from the 1990 census are likely to show an even lower figure. The compositions of households in the United States have changed greatly. About 71 percent of all households in 1990 were family households, compared with 74 percent in 1980. The changes in household type between 1980 and 1990 is shown in Table 3 (on page 5).

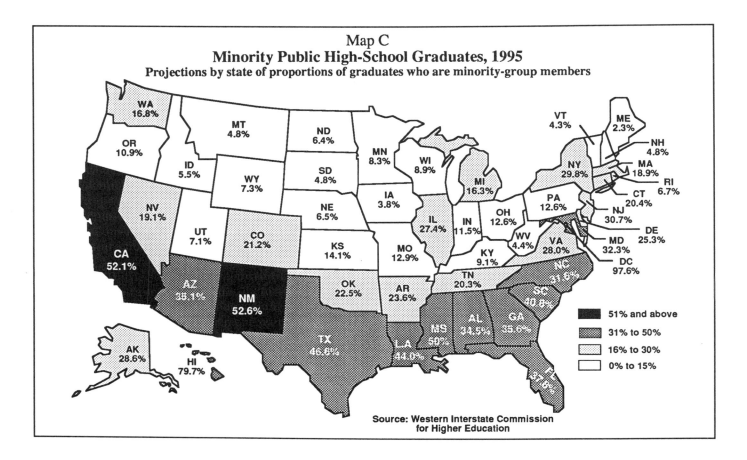

Map C
Minority Public High-School Graduates, 1995
Projections by state of proportions of graduates who are minority-group members

Source: Western Interstate Commission
for Higher Education

These changes in households mean that 52 million households contain a married couple, and 41 million don't. By the next census, the numbers will be about equal. In 1990, according to data from the U.S. Census Bureau, only about one household in three contained a child (under age 18) and <u>less than 20 percent</u> of all households (17 million) had one or more children of school age (ages 6 to 17 years).

A few other notable changes which occurred during the 1980s are listed below.

♦ 82 percent of all children (under age 18) now have working mothers and six of ten mothers of preschool-age children (under age 6) work outside the home at least part-time.

♦ Women who are single parents are raising 13.7 million children with a median family income of $10,982 (as of 1989). If the children are living with two adults, the median family income

increases to $36,872. Forecasters say that sixty percent of today's children will live with a single parent at some time before they reach age 18; in 1990, 1.2 million men were raising kids by themselves, compared to 6.6 million women; and over three million children are being raised by their grandparents.

♦ Over one million young mothers (age 20-24) could not work or look for work in 1986 because they could not find quality or affordable child care.

♦ In 1990, 13 percent of all children were regularly hungry, 25 percent were born to unmarried parents, over 20 percent of all children under age 18 were poor, about 350,000 children were born to drug-addicted mothers, 19 percent had no health insurance, and 166 juveniles of every 100,000 were behind bars.

Table 3 Change in Household Type, U.S. 1980 - 1990		
	1980-90 % Change	Number of Hshlds (000) 1990
Total Households	+15.5%	93,347
Married couples, no children*	+15.0%	27,780
Married couples, w/children*	-1.7%	24,537
Single parent* - women	+21.2%	6,599
Single parent* -men	+87.2%	1,153
Singles living alone	+25.7%	22,999
Singles living with non-relatives	+45.3%	4,258

*Children under age 18
Source: U.S. Bureau of the Census, Current Population Survey, Household and Family Characteristics.

♦ The number one goal of the President and Governor's "Education Summit" is to ensure that every child enters kindergarten healthy, well-fed and from a supportive home environment. Given the data presented above, it is no surprise that the cost of achieving this goal would be over $40 billion.

♦ Most Americans now live in our 39 largest metropolitan areas, mostly in the suburbs.

♦ Sixty-four percent of all new jobs created in the last decade were in the suburbs. As a result, the most common commute is from a suburban HOME to a suburban JOB.

♦ In 1988, 57 percent of the nation's families and individuals could not qualify to buy a median-priced home in the area where they lived.

A LOOK AHEAD: WE GROW, BUT MORE SLOWLY

Looking out to the year 2000 and beyond, we can see some interesting shifts. The total U.S. population continues to increase, but at a slower rate, up to 267.7 million in 2000 (7.1 percent), and up to 282.2 million in 2010, (only 5.3 percent). However, America's youth population (age 0-17) goes up from 64.4 million in 1990 to 67.4 million in 2000, then DECLINES to 64.9 million in 2010, according to Census Bureau projections. This decline is already foreseeable in the decline in the number of females moving into the child-bearing years. Fewer women producing fewer children seems a safe hypothesis. The decline will be in the number of white youth particularly as is shown in Table 4.

Table 4 Projections of the U.S. Population Age 0 - 17, 1990 - 2010			
	(millions)		
Youth	1990	2010	Change
Total youth*	64.4	64.9	+0.5
White, non-Hispanic	45.2	41.4	-3.8
Hispanic (of any race)	7.2	9.8	+2.6
Black**	10.2	11.4	+1.2
Other Races**	2.2	2.8	+0.6
INCREASE IN TOTAL NONWHITE YOUTH +4.4 MILLION			
DECREASE IN TOTAL WHITE YOUTH -3.8 MILLION			

*May not add exactly because of rounding.
**Includes small number of Hispanics; "other races" are primarily Asian and Native American.
Source: U.S. Census Bureau as cited in National Center for Education Statistics, Youth Indicators 1991.

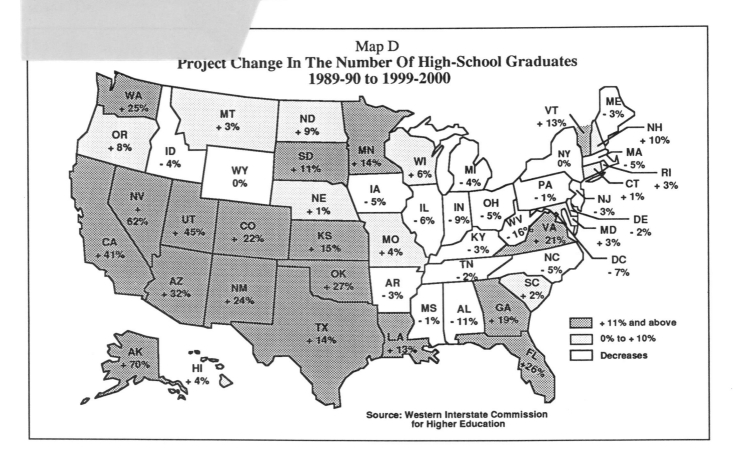

Map D
**Project Change In The Number Of High-School Graduates
1989-90 to 1999-2000**

+ 11% and above
0% to + 10%
Decreases

Source: Western Interstate Commission
for Higher Education

A key rule of demographics is, if you weren't born, you don't count. It's silly to mourn the loss of 3.8 million white youth. As pragmatists, we must ensure that the additional 4.4 million nonwhite young people get the best education and access to good jobs as we possibly can, for the nation's health, and also because they will be funding our Social Security payments!

If the U.S. population is increasing all through the next two decades but the youth populations decline after 2000, it means that the nation's average age will go up like a rocket after 2000. The eldest baby boomers, now 46, will begin to retire in droves after 2000. The baby boomlet is now working its way through junior high, but half of this increase in youth is in California, Texas and Florida. There is no boomlet in most heartland and mid-Atlantic states as Map D (above) makes clear.

"Minority" Peoples In 2010

By 2010, 12 states (listed in Table 5) plus the District of Columbia will have significant minority youth populations. About half of the nation's 64.4 million young people will reside in these 12 states. The question that arises from this situation is *what should we call "minorities" when they are more than half of the population?* In 26 cities in California in 1990, no single racial or ethnic group made up a majority of the population. As a result, no elections could be won by any single racial or ethnic group including whites. Coalition politics was the only winning pattern.

Concentrations of Nonwhite Youth

We normally think of "high minority" states as being in the deep south. That was true in 1940, as blacks were, for all practical purposes, the only

Table 5 Percent Nonwhite Youth* Projections for 2010 for Selected States			
State	Percent Nonwhite	State	Percent Nonwhite
D.C.	93.2%	Louisiana	50.3%
Hawaii	79.5%	Mississippi	49.9%
Texas	56.9%	New Jersey	45.7
California	56.9%	Maryland	42.7%
Florida	53.4%	Illinois	41.7%
New York	52.8%	South Carolina	40.1%
U.S.	38.2%		

*Age 0 - 17 years.
Source: U.S. Census Bureau as cited in American Demographics, May 1989.

statistically significant minority group. Since about 1970, the process has been one of making America more ethnically diverse. Looking at the list of states in Table 5 (above), one sees many of our largest and most politically powerful states as well as some states in the deep south. In New York, California, Texas and Florida, each racial and ethnic group is expanding, beginning with the youngest portion of each group. By 2010, these FOUR states will contain 21 million of the nation's total 64.4 million youth, one-third of all youth (age 0 to 17) in the U.S. (New York is a special case. Although youth in New York will decline from 4.2 million in 1990 to 3.8 million in 2010, the decline is virtually among the white group. New York still remains a very large and powerful state.) As the nonwhite youth majority moves through the age range in these four key states, we will see first a majority of entry level workers, new households, new parents, promotions, voters, volunteers, semi-retirees and finally minority Social Security recipients, in that order.

Fertility and Class

It is hard to see what realistically would be likely to increase the white fertility rate in the U.S. (or in Europe). Given that 70 percent of all women of childbearing-age are in the work force, deferring fertility as late as possible in order to keep two incomes in the family (for those married women and one income for single women), the notion that vast numbers of women will give up their jobs, return to their homes and dedicate themselves to the raising of three or more children (or even one) is science fiction -- the loss of their income would be catastrophic for most households.

Indeed, as more minorities enter the middle class, we see a decline in their fertility as well. Middle class families have by definition some discretionary income, if that surplus is distributed among eight children, each share will be too small to do much, but if there are only one or two children, the surplus could change the children's lives. A report by the Business-Higher Education Forum indicated that in 1987, 36 percent of black families and 40 percent of Hispanic families are middle class - with incomes of $25,000 or more. A 1991 report by the Census Bureau using a measure called "relative income" that takes family size into consideration found that more than half of all black and Hispanic persons had middle incomes in 1989 (51 and 55 percent respectively). Asian Americans also have a large middle income group, due to increased education and having several workers in each household. In Los Angeles, Washington, D.C., Miami, Newark and Atlanta, a MAJORITY of black residents were living in the suburbs in 1990, a clear indicator of middle class membership. Show me a minority child raised in a suburb and whose parents are college graduates, and I will show you a child whose educational performance is roughly the same as that of a white child raised in a suburb by parents who are college graduates. For example, Figure 1 (on page 8) indicates the math performance of eighth-graders of each ethnic group, comparing the richest quarter of each group with the poorest. Much of what looks like race is really class.

Uneven Minority Distribution

We also need to remember that with this increased national diversity, 11 states in 1990 had 10 percent or LESS nonwhite in their youth population. Maine moves from 2.8 percent

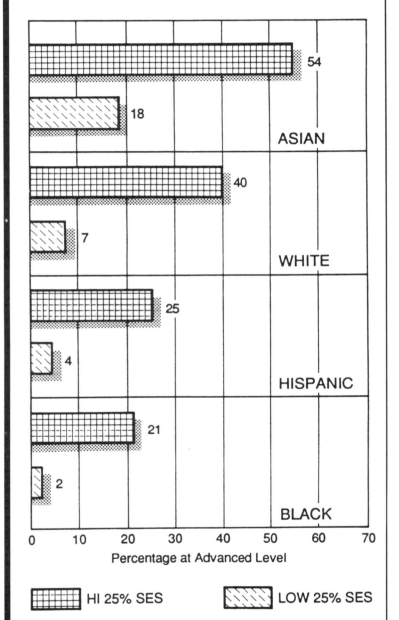

Figure 1
Percentage of Eighth Graders in Low and High Socioeconomic Groups Who Are Proficient in Advanced Mathematics, by Race and Ethnicity, 1988

Percentage at Advanced Level

ASIAN — 54, 18
WHITE — 40, 7
HISPANIC — 25, 4
BLACK — 21, 2

HI 25% SES   LOW 25% SES

Source: National Center for Education Statistics, National Education Longitudinal Study of 1988, A Profile of the American Eighth Grader, 1990.

nonwhite youth in 1990 to 3.1 percent in 2010, Vermont from 2.4 percent in 1990 to 5.4 percent in 2010. (See Appendix Table A -- Projections of the Minority Youth Population). Thus, states will become much more *unlike* in terms of ethnic diversity over the next twenty years. Youth will be more concentrated in a smaller number of states. By 2010, 32.6 million of the nation's 62.6 million children will be in only nine states: Texas, California, Florida, New York, Illinois, Georgia, Michigan, Ohio and Pennsylvania. Some will have little ethnic diversity - Pennsylvania goes from 16.1 percent nonwhite in 1990 to 18.7 percent in 2010, Ohio from 16.2 percent to 20.8 percent. Ohio and Pennsylvania also will decline in total youth during the 1990 to 2010 period, while California, Texas and Florida will gain 1.8 million youth. Over half of the youth population in these three states will be nonwhite well before 2010.

IMPLICATIONS FOR EDUCATION

Slums and Suburbs

Given that minorities are more likely to be in poverty than whites (most poor kids are white, although black and Hispanic kids have a much higher percentage of their total number poor) and given our look at the future, we might ask how schools are likely to fare with the clientele we have isolated. The best guess would be -- *reasonably well*. Although the conventional wisdom in 1991 was that ALL schools were terrible, the evidence for that view is very thin. The top 15 percent of America's students are world class on any set of indicators. The "forgotten middle" needs some work, but will graduate from high school and pay taxes. America's lowest 35 percent (in terms of school attainment) is truly awful, due to factors that were present when they first knocked on the kindergarten door. (Factors such as: poverty, out of wedlock birth, teen births, cocaine-addicted at birth, short of food and housing, born premature, are only a few.) America's best schools (and students) are located in the suburbs of our 40 largest metropolitan areas;

the worst schools are located in the inner cities of the same metro areas plus some rural areas.

If one looks for the schools that most need assistance from state and federal governments, it is clearly our inner city schools and even easier to ignore rural ones. But now that MOST VOTERS live in the suburbs, it is easier for most political leaders to ignore inner city schools. (For example, AMERICA 2000: An Education Strategy announced by President Bush, never mentions reduction of poverty in inner city schools as a major educational task for the nation.) Many of these inner city schools are performing heroically, against all the odds. However, if the suburbs continue to suck jobs, income, housing, shopping, churches, restaurants, colleges and corporate headquarters away from their core cities, there is a danger that inner city schools could become a real socio-economic dumping ground in the next 20 years.

It is also clear from our analyses that states will differ even more in the number of students and the diversity of those students, and perhaps even in educational attainment in the years to come. Coupled with the amazing changes that have taken place in the American family over the last decade, early childhood prevention programs like Head Start will be even more essential in the future. Yet, as of this writing Head Start programs are reaching less than half of all eligible children.

Preparing for Diversity
We are already beginning to see the power of some of the nation's largest and most rapidly growing states in areas like textbook adoptions for schools, with the influence of California and Texas in areas like history, social studies and science. These two states represented almost one-fifth of all the textbook adoptions in the nation in 1991, and will represent more than one-fifth in 2010. Add Florida, and you approach one-third of all textbook adoptions. Yet, in all three states, the makeup of the legislatures is not yet representative of the racial and ethnic diversity of the citizens. Neither is the makeup of teachers. While over half of all students in these three states will be nonwhite in 2010, about 19 percent of the teaching staff in California, 15 percent in Florida and 22 percent in Texas will be nonwhite. This is based on who is currently preparing to become teachers in

schools of education. These three states also have among the highest high school dropout rates in the nation. *Who will assist new white teachers in discovering what their diverse students are like?*

Who Will Do the Work?
There is currently a major debate about jobs in the year 2000, but no debate about who the entry-level workers will be. (The NEW workers in 2000 will be 85 percent combinations of immigrants, women and minorities. About 15 percent of new workers will be white males, according to the Hudson Institute's Workforce 2000 report. That's a net figure.) The debate centers around the work to be done. Some analysts are insisting that in a high-tech age, MOST jobs will require a college degree. However, the most authoritative judgement, from an excellent Carnegie study: America's Choice: High Skills Or Low Wages, is that in 2000, 70 percent of America's jobs will not require a college degree.

The best guess is that we are creating two work forces: one in minimum wage occupations that can be performed by high school dropouts, such as janitor, clerk, fast food worker, hotel room maid, and the other in well-paid occupations in technical or administrative positions that need a college degree for entry. What has been declining throughout America are jobs in the middle of the economic range. In 1991, for every new job created for a computer programmer, 11 new jobs for clerks were created or eight new jobs for food service workers or six new jobs for janitors. This leads to an "information-rich" and "information-poor" split in our society. These two sets of predictions (shown in Table 6, next page) of jobs for 2000 makes the point. Health technology is growing most rapidly, but that number of jobs is dwarfed by the number of low-end service jobs. The service work force has a small "middle" and a large number of high and low paying jobs at the extremes.

Given that minorities are such a large percentage of the new workers in the next 20 years, there are three possibilities that can happen:

Table 6 Fastest Growing Jobs, 1988 - 2000		
Job:	% Increase	Total Jobs in 2000
Paralegal	75.3%	145,000
Medical Asst.	70.0%	253,000
Radiologic Technician	66.0%	218,000
Largest Number of Jobs in 2000:		
Salesclerks		4,564,000
Janitor/maid		3,450,000
Waiter/Waitress		2,337,000
Source: U.S. Department of Labor, Monthly Labor Review, November 1989.		

1. If more minorities graduate from high school and take some community college course training, 1.2 million new health technology jobs will be waiting.

2. If minorities drop out of high school, 4.2 million new service jobs will be waiting, of which three million are minimum wage and can be done by high school dropouts. (Minorities are now over-represented in this job category.)

3. If minorities go to college and graduate, 3.5 million new professional jobs (lawyers, doctors, teachers, accountants, etc.) will be waiting. (Minorities are now under-represented in these fields.)

Given the recent evidence from the Census Bureau confirming the increased number of rich and poor households in our nation, and the decline of middle-income households, it seems that the nation would benefit if more minorities opted for options one and three, with clear access to the middle class and the fulfillment of "the American Dream."

Mickey Mouse, Star Wars and Equity

Our three "megastates" of Florida, Texas and California have one thing in common: tourism is the biggest industry in all three, with "tech" a clear second. For every person who works for General Motors, there are about three people who work for McDonald's. Those in tourism hire clerks, waiters/waitresses, janitors and maids. Most new workers in these three states will be nonwhite. The equity issues involve access, through education and jobs, to a middle class status. It seems unlikely that these three states will be able to INCREASE access to the middle class for their dominant minority populations during the next 20 years. The result is likely to be social tension over the next 20 years based less on race and ethnicity and more on the combination of age, class and race. (Do we want to give every BLACK child a shot at a good education today, given that some black children have millionaire parents, or do we want to focus on giving every POOR child a head start?)

It may be time to take the issue of wealth and class head on as a major focus of our continuing debate about equity. Since the 1960s, we have been devoted to a single equity mission - the racial desegregation of schools. Desegregation of jobs and housing were afterthoughts during the 1960s with daily reminders that the task of desegregation is not progressing. Because large numbers of minorities (read blacks) were poor in 1960, desegregating schools meant equalizing access to the middle class. Today's strategy is different, as many minority families have moved into the middle class.

We realize that the young people most at risk of not achieving their potential are young people in POVERTY, regardless of race.

Thus, the courts have declared that the Kentucky educational system was unlawful, because poor small school districts were spending much less per child than rich school districts, resulting in the Kentucky Education Reform Act. Texas, Virginia and many other states have encountered similar suits. **If you are concerned about the scores of U.S. students compared to the scores of Asian students, try looking at the scores of U.S. inner city students compared to the scores of suburban students.**

How Do We Govern Metropolitan Areas?

The most obvious inequities in 1992 are those of the inner city and the surrounding suburbs. The difference in educational spending between these two areas are, if anything, more spectacular than those between states. The difference is that there is no governing body designed to deal with metropolitan areas where most Americans now live. Geographical distance leads to social distance. How do we get wealthy suburbanites to take seriously the problems of the city they fled to get to suburbia in the first place? **What would it take to get middle income people to move back to the inner city?** During the last decade the walls between city and suburb were built even thicker to insulate the suburbanites from any real contact with the problems of the inner city. During the 1990s and beyond, inner city problems like crime, drugs, poverty, youth violence, and family disruption will begin to move past the walls of the inner city into the suburbs. At that moment perhaps, suburban residents will realize that equity is a vital pragmatic goal and that their lives will improve if inner city residents have access to a good education and a good job.

> An equitable society must be concerned about a variety of areas - race, sex, class, geographic region and age, **and** how these areas interrelate in people's lives.

Ask me to take you to a place where whites, blacks, Hispanics, Asians and Native Americans live together in peace and harmony and I can take you to any number of places. But if you ask me to take you to a place where rich and poor people live together in peace and harmony, I will answer that there is no such place. Much of what appears to be a problem between races is actually a problem between classes. It may well be that recognition of the need to make class differences more permeable for those who are willing to work hard and accept the challenge of the American Dream is the final and most difficult frontier of the equity journey for America.

A SCENARIO FOR THE NEXT TWO DECADES

T he population of the world moves past six billion, India becomes the largest nation in the world, eclipsing China, the West (U.S. and all its NATO allies) move from being 18 percent of the world's people to being less than 10 percent, Caucasians will be about 10 percent of the world's population. At this level, the West can "lead" the world, but not by military conquest. (It's hard to occupy the territory where 90 percent of the world lives.) In 1992, it became clear that the sperm count for Western men had dropped dramatically, meaning that about one man in five would be unable to become a father. This then would accelerate the decline of Western populations. The Newly Industrialized Countries (NICs) will have developed sizeable middle class populations with discretionary income, which means that their fertility rates will go down while the large groups in poverty will continue to reproduce at a higher rate. This conflict between the better-educated middle class and the poverty groups will become a major source of tensions in these countries. While the number of HIV cases will continue to rise, the rise will not be exponential, and AIDS will not become the leading cause of death in the world, although it may be in Sub-Saharan Africa.

The U.S. will continue to grow, but at less than the 9.8 percent rate of the 1980 to 1990 period. After 2010, the population will begin to stabilize, and after 2020, immigration will become a major source of new human beings for the United States, and will be responsible for whatever growth occurs in the U.S. population after about 2030. The U. S. will continue to attract about two-thirds of the world's immigration, (particularly after Europe begins to stabilize). The U.S. will continue to get 85 percent of its immigrants from Central and South America.

Growth will be concentrated in nonwhite populations, in the south and west, and in the suburbs of our 40 largest metro areas. "Edge Cities" - self-contained suburbs outside the metro center - will become common, leading to further destruction of the inner cities as money, talent, education and jobs continue their move to the suburbs and Edge Cities. The problem of attracting middle classes of whatever racial and ethnic group back to the inner cities to live will prove a most intractable one. More black, Asian and Hispanic suburban populations will be seen. Some increase in growth will happen in the heartland states like Minnesota and Michigan, particularly after Michigan diversifies its economy away from auto manufacturing, as is already happening now.

Some of the "big nine" states that now contain half of the U.S. population will be eclipsed by the "new south:" Georgia, North Carolina, Virginia, adding to the racial and ethnic mix in our biggest states. New York will remain big and powerful but drops to third in size as Texas moves to number two by 2000. With all the increase in racial and ethnic diversity in the nation, there will be little increase in diversity in the New England states, which will remain 10 percent nonwhite. Thus, the states will become more UNlike in terms of size and diversity, creating a concentration of power in the House of Representatives that will be uncommon - California, Texas and Florida will gain in clout.

By 2000, we will have almost as many households without a married couple as there will be with a married couple. In 2002, the oldest "baby-boomers, now age 46, become 55, and will begin to retire. (Many of them are planning to leave the work force early). As life expectancy increases, a large number of people will work for 30 years (age 25 to 55) and will be retired for 30 years (age 55 to 85) giving them one year of retirement for every year of work. That will put an impossible burden on the Social Security system. In 1950 there were 18 workers to share the costs of each retiree; in 2035, there will be only TWO workers to support each retiree. While the youth population (age 0 - 17 years) shrink from 34 percent of the U.S. population in 1970 to 25 percent in 2000, we move

from 20 million people over age 65 in 1970 to 40 million in 2000 and 65 million in 2030.

Older people vote more often than younger ones and they are increasingly unlikely to support education or youth-related programs at state and federal levels. In 2030, the work force that supports the (still very white) elderly population will be about half white and the younger workers will be about 60 percent "minority" and female. Elderly minority populations will become more frequent, particularly in the middle class populations. Prisons will deal with more elderly prisoners on life support systems, as their life sentences are non-commutable.

By 2010, the job structure in the U.S. will be even more two-tailed, with about 30 to 40 percent of all jobs requiring a college education and paying very well, while 30 percent or more will continue to be "working poor" jobs for high school dropouts. We will continue to develop one new job for a computer programmer for every seven new jobs for clerks/cashiers. Tourism, our largest industry, will continue to grow and will contribute a large number of "working poor" jobs. As pointed out earlier, this separation will lead to "information-rich" and "information-poor" segments of our society, which is closely tied to wealth.

As the 40 largest metro areas continue to attract people and jobs, the viability of rural life will come into question shortly after 2000. (Almost half of U.S. counties lost population between 1980 and 1990. Over 90 percent of Iowa's counties did). The provision of medical and social services to sparse and declining populations will be as costly as providing them to inner city populations, and the "rural underclass" may rival the "urban underclass" as a problem area. However, the suburban majority, worried about the incursion of poverty and violence from inner cities, will try to keep the focus placed on the urban underclass.

The federal government will continue to find itself unable to lead the nation (it is too big for the small problems and too small for the big problems), allowing leadership to go, by default, to state and local governments and organizations. The wave of collaborative alliances (between education and health particularly) seen in the 1990s should continue for several decades, as local success stories begin to increase and people participate locally to further their self-interest. (Even in our earliest voluntary associations, the barn-raising benefitted everyone eventually. Liberals and pragmatists both came.) More effort was placed on the local PREVENTION of social and medical problems, rather than their expensive and ineffective "cures."

By about 2010, most Americans should come to see that as the number of children continue to decline as a percent of the U.S. population, we cannot afford to throw any child away. (One cannot be a rising economy with a falling population.) The neglect of one-third of youth, common throughout the 1980s, will be seen as being contrary to the nation's interest, particularly the local community. Minority middle class groups will begin to apply pressure in these areas as well as whites. By the same token, metropolitan planning authorities should begin to increase in number and influence and begin to coordinate the interests of the increasingly affluent suburbs with that of the core city that spawned them in the first place. With such a new governing mechanism, some of the problems of an increasingly divided society may finally begin to be dealt with effectively. This may seem optimistic, but the only alternative is the destruction of America's core cities. Tomorrow is indeed an extension of today's trends.

MAJOR SOURCES USED IN THIS REPORT

American Association of Colleges for Teacher Education, <u>Teacher Education Pipeline: Schools, Colleges, and Departments of Education Enrollments by Race and Ethnicity</u>. Washington, D.C.: 1988.

<u>American Demographics</u>, "All Our Children," May 1989.

<u>American Demographics</u>, "How Children Are Changing," February 1992.

Business-Higher Education Forum, <u>Three Realities: Minority Life in the United States</u>. Washington, D.C.: 1990.

Carnegie Center on Education and the Economy. <u>America's Choice: High Skills or Low Wages</u>, New York: 1990.

Cendata. The U.S. Census Bureau's on-line database, accessed through CompuServe.

U.S. Bureau of the Census, Economics and Statistics Administration, "1990 Census Profile: Race and Hispanic Origin," Number 2, June 1991.

_____. <u>Household and Family Characteristics, March 1990 and 1989</u>, Washington, D.C.: Government Printing Office, December 1990.

_____. <u>Projections of the Population of States by Age, Sex and Race: 1989 to 2010</u>. Washington, D.C.: Government Printing Office, January 1990.

_____. <u>Statistical Abstract of the United States, 1991</u>. Washington, D.C.: Government Printing Office, 1991.

_____. <u>Trends in Relative Income: 1964 to 1989</u>, Washington, D.C.: Government Printing Office, December 1991.

U.S. Department of Education, National Center for Education Statistics, <u>National Education Longitudinal Study of 1988, A Profile of the American Eighth Grader</u>. Washington, D.C.: Government Printing Office, 1990.

U.S. Department of Education, Office of Educational Research and Improvement, <u>Youth Indicators 1991: Trends in Well-Being of American Youth</u>. Washington, D.C.: Government Printing Office, April 1991.

Western Interstate Commission for Higher Education and The College Board, <u>The Road To College: Educational Progress by Race and Ethnicity</u>. Boulder: Western Interstate Commission for Higher Education, July 1991.

APPENDIX

Total Children Under Age 18 and Minority* Youth As A Percent of the Total Youth Population by State 1990 and Projections for 2000 and 2010 (Ranked by Percent Minority in 2010)						
	1990		2000		2010	
State	Total Children Under Age 18 (000)	Percent Minority	Total Children Under Age 18 (000)	Percent Minority	Total Children Under Age 18 (000)	Percent Minority
United States	63,604	31.1	65,717	34.0	62,644	38.2
District of Columbia	117	87.2	111	90.9	105	93.2
Hawaii	280	72.5	296	76.4	310	79.5
New Mexico	447	60.2	569	70.0	595	76.5
Texas	4,836	49.1	5,415	51.9	5,418	56.9
California	7,751	54.1	8,402	51.4	8,520	56.9
Florida	2,866	36.2	3,244	48.6	3,270	53.4
New York	4,260	37.9	4,189	45.8	3,862	52.8
Louisiana	1,227	41.6	1,229	47.3	1,118	50.3
Mississippi	747	46.7	791	48.8	749	49.9
New Jersey	1,799	33.1	2,037	40.2	1,935	45.7
Maryland	1,162	35.8	1,267	40.2	1,220	42.7
Illinois	2,946	32.7	2,947	36.8	2,684	41.7
South Carolina	920	39.8	968	39.6	931	40.1
Georgia	1,727	36.7	2,056	36.4	2,116	37.9
Arizona	981	40.3	1,191	33.6	1,229	37.1
Delaware	163	26.8	179	32.9	177	37.0
Alabama	1,059	34.2	1,111	34.8	1,046	35.6
Nevada	297	28.0	286	30.0	288	33.4
North Carolina	1,606	31.9	1,723	32.3	1,684	33.2
Colorado	861	25.4	924	28.9	893	33.1
Alaska	172	31.7	201	29.5	208	32.7
Virginia	1,505	28.7	1,607	29.4	1,549	31.1
Michigan	2,459	22.3	2,347	25.5	2,094	29.2
Oklahoma	837	25.7	838	24.8	795	**27.5**
Connecticut	750	23.4	781	23.4	715	**27.0**
Arkansas	621	24.3	621	26.1	576	**26.8**

-continued-

	1990		2000		2010	
State	Total Children Under Age 18 (000)	Percent Minority	Total Children Under Age 18 (000)	Percent Minority	Total Children Under Age 18 (000)	Percent Minority
Tennessee	1,217	22.5	1,204	24.1	1,125	25.3
Ohio	2,800	16.2	2,631	18.6	2,349	20.8
Wyoming	136	11.8	137	17.8	125	20.2
Missouri	1,315	16.6	1,331	18.5	1,236	19.9
South Dakota	198	13.9	193	16.2	180	19.8
Washington	1,261	17.9	1,163	16.9	1,098	19.5
Kansas	662	15.3	633	17.1	585	19.3
Indiana	1,456	13.3	1,382	16.7	1,242	19.2
Pennsylvania	2,795	16.1	2,609	16.7	2,260	18.7
Rhode Island	226	16.3	236	15.5	222	18.6
Massachusetts	1,353	17.9	1,368	15.5	1,267	18.2
Oregon	724	12.8	677	14.1	637	16.8
Wisconsin	1,289	13.5	1,208	13.7	1,067	16.6
Montana	222	12.0	198	13.2	181	15.4
Kentucky	954	10.2	906	12.6	818	14.1
Nebraska	429	10.4	398	10.8	358	13.1
Utah	627	9.7	715	11.2	740	12.4
Minnesota	1,167	9.8	1,138	9.1	1,042	11.2
Idaho	308	10.1	291	9.4	275	11.0
North Dakota	175	9.1	157	8.6	138	10.0
Iowa	719	5.8	622	7.0	529	8.7
West Virginia	444	4.9	401	6.7	344	7.3
New Hampshire	279	3.4	329	4.8	317	5.5
Vermont	143	2.4	150	4.7	138	5.4
Maine	309	2.8	310	3.0	284	3.1

Total Children Under Age 18 and Minority* Youth As A Percent of the Total Youth Population by State 1990 and Projections for 2000 and 2010 (Ranked by Percent Minority in 2010)

*Minority include blacks, Asians and Pacific Islanders, Native Americans and Alaskan Natives, and other races as well as white Hispanics. The projections for all minorities were derived by American Demographics.

Source: 1990 - Bureau of the Census; and 2000 and 2010 projections from "Projections of the Population of States by Age, Sex and Race: 1988 to 2010," by Signe I. Wetrogen, Bureau of the Census as cited in American Demographics, May 1989.

Selected Publications from IEL's Center for Demographic Policy*

The Demographics of American Indians: One Percent of the Population, Fifty Percent of the Diversity by Harold L. Hodgkinson, Janice Hamilton Outtz, Anita M. Obarakpor-1990-26 pp.-$12.00

The authors give a short but comprehensive look at the American Indian population. Topic areas include: How many are there? Where do they live? What is the educational status? Are there major differences between the top ten states? Also included is a look at the major tribes.

The Same Client: The Demographics of Education and Service Delivery Systems by Harold L. Hodgkinson-1989-28 pp.-$12.00

"Educators at all levels need to begin to become familiar with other service providers at their level, as they are serving the same children and families as clients. This report calls for collaboration between organizations providing services in the areas of education, transportation, health, housing and corrections.

Demographic State Profiles by Harold L. Hodgkinson-$7.00

These reports on 24 individual states and local areas have focused on demographic trends confronting state and local-level policy makers now or in the future. For a list of state reports available or for information on getting an analysis for your state, please contact us.

CDP Demographics for Decision-Makers newsletter. Beginning in September 1992, the Center's Demographics for Education quarterly newsletter is expanding its focus and will become available to a wider group of decision-makers. **For $250 annually to organizations or $75 to individuals,** the newsletter is a cost-effective way to keep aware of major demographic issues. The trends identified make evident the need for collaboration among diverse organizations in all sectors. Whether you are providing services, planning programs or just trying to understand how things are changing, this newsletter is for you. The newsletter will be available on or about the 15th of September, December, March and June. To subscribe, please fill out the form below and return it. For more information, please call (202) 822-8405.

☐ **Yes**, I want to be informed on how things are changing demographically so that I can make better decisions. Sign me up for a one-year subscription!

☐ Organizational Subscription (My check for $250 is enclosed.)
☐ Individual Subscription (My personal check for $75 is enclosed.)

_____
(Your Name, please type or print)

_____
(Mailing Address: where you want the newsletter sent)

_____
(City, State and zip code)

_____
(area code and phone number)

*A complete list of publications is available from the Institute for Educational Leadership upon request.